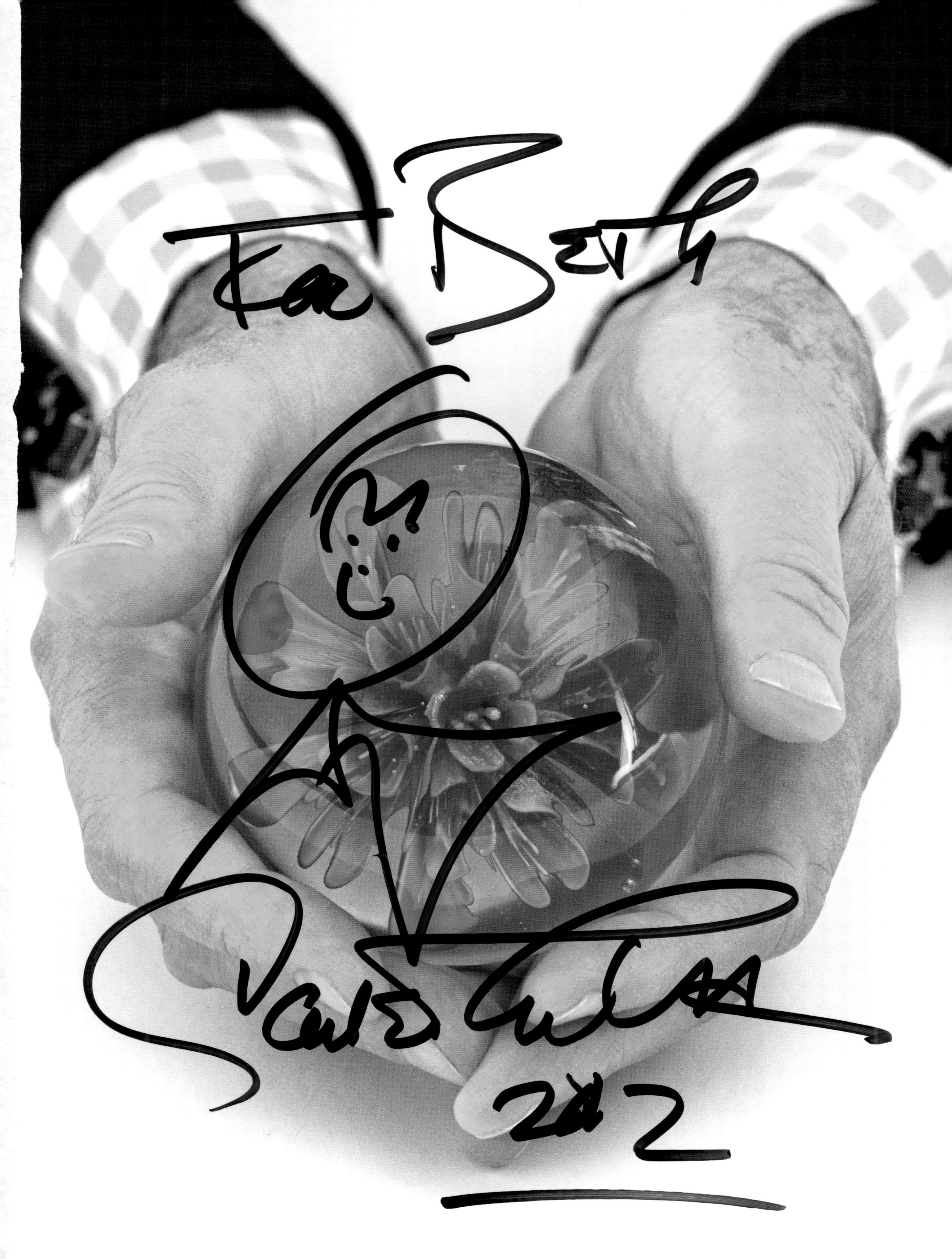
For Beth
2012

Mr. Color

THE GREENBRIER AND OTHER DECORATING ADVENTURES

CARLETON VARNEY

PROJECT COORDINATOR: BRINSLEY MATTHEWS

DESIGN: JOEL AVIROM

EDITORIAL DIRECTOR: JANE K. CREECH

COPY EDITOR: ANNE HELLMAN WHITE

RESEARCH: NELLIE XINOS

PHOTOGRAPHS BY MICHEL ARNAUD

SHANNONGROVE PRESS

NEW YORK

CONTENTS

Foreword

GROWING UP, MY FAMILY CONSIDERED the Greenbrier to be the Emerald City. I remember the first time I stepped inside as a child. All of the bright colors and flowers made me think I had just landed in Oz, and I was awestruck. I had never seen anything so vibrant and colorful in my whole life and couldn't believe there was something this magnificent in West Virginia. Little did I know then how incredibly talented the Greenbrier's decorator was. Thankfully, in 2009, I had the opportunity to meet Carleton Varney, the president of Dorothy Draper and Company, Inc., and the man responsible for maintaining the hotel's iconic, color-filled interiors.

When we first met, I was the new owner of the resort, and we had just announced plans for a casino, retail corridor, and additional restaurants. Upon hearing Carleton's passion for the Draper look and how integral those designs are to the soul of the resort, I knew his ideas were more than just bright colors and bold prints: they epitomized the rebirth of the Greenbrier that we wanted to create. Today, our Casino Club is an elegant and sophisticated entertainment venue unlike any I've ever seen. In fact, noted columnist Cindy Adams called it "the most beautiful casino in the world."

Carleton's sense of style and keen inspiration did not end with the Casino Club. He completely renovated our arrival foyer and registration area, maintaining key elements such as the Springhouse and Zuber panoramas, all the while creating more open and welcoming spaces. Carleton used his exceptional talents and extraordinary palette of colors, fabrics, and designs to transform every corner and hallway into a masterpiece.

Carleton loves this grand resort as much as I do. In one of our earliest conversations, he shared with me his thoughts about the Greenbrier's Draper décor. As he explained it: "The Greenbrier is unlike any other place in the world. When you leave many hotels and a friend asks you to describe your room, you may not be able to remember the decoration because of its decided blandness. When you leave the Greenbrier and are asked to describe your room, I do think you'll be able to recall the big red roses with green leaves on the walls, bright-green carpeting, Thomas Jefferson–blue drapery, and scarlet club chairs. Whether your room has wallpaper of yellow roses or pink falling tulips or some other garden flower of the Allegheny Mountains, I am certain you will be aware of its existence."

When drawing up the schemes, Carleton, like his mentor Dorothy Draper, maintained an eye toward comfort and old-fashioned hospitality. Whether crafting the designs for a restaurant or the Greenbrier Presidential Express, our new twenty-car steam-engine train, Carleton's outstanding ability to reinvigorate the Greenbrier's signature feel was evident. That style continues to attract and impress resort guests generation after generation.

Carleton is one of the most internationally celebrated interior designers in the world. He rejects the impractical, uncomfortable, and bland and embraces the fearless, whimsical, and vivid. Although he works magic in celebrity homes as well as royal palaces, I know how much the Greenbrier means to him. For more than forty years, his passion and talents have been synonymous with this national treasure, and I am proud to see that wonderful tradition continue. For, as the Greenbrier's future evolves, one thing is certain: Carleton Varney will be there.

Jim Justice

OPPOSITE: Café Carleton is the name Jim Justice gave to this carefree restaurant and coffee shop at the resort. The café is decorated in red, red, red, with black and gold accents. The orchestra mural was hand painted by Susan Kent. The banquettes and Dorothy Draper chairs are upholstered in a red-on-red, cut-relief velvet fabric from Carleton V Ltd., and the custom red-swirl carpet was designed by Brinsley Matthews as a melody all its own.

Living with color changes your life, and my life has been a colorful one. I grew up in Nahant, Massachusetts, in a white house with green shutters and interiors bathed in red, green, blue, yellow, even orange. My sister Vivian and I were given boxes of Crayola crayons and coloring books at an early age. I still remember spending hours filling in the cottage where Little Red Riding Hood's grandmother lived, a gingerbread house, and images of castles as I saw fit. Years later, destiny would bring real-life castles and palaces for me to decorate: from Dromoland Castle in County Clare, Ireland, to, most recently, the Royal Palace of Lithuania in Vilnius.

I am happiest when surrounded by color. In decorating, I believe in a strong use of honest color, and the numerous hotels, restaurants, and private residences for which I have composed interiors demonstrate this philosophy. A number of my clients call me Mr. Color.

Over the course of forty years in the business, I have discovered that people simply do not see color as I do and often shy away from it. When I first started my career at Dorothy Draper and Company, Inc., as a junior decorator in the 1960s, Mrs. Draper would walk around the office peering over our shoulders. Her now-famous mantra was, "Show me no gravy." She did not want to see a gray or beige scheme on our drafting tables. That was my training! A Draper decorator is all about color.

I believe there is a perfect color for every person. There is a red personality, a yellow personality. I am a green man. I love to sit in a room with rich palm-tree-green-painted walls, feeling as though I am lounging on a hammock in a tropical garden. With a deep-green background, I will use any color I like for the ceiling, upholstery, drapery, and carpeting. I also love to combine green with red. Some say I decorate with Christmas colors. But why do we only use color at holiday time? The sparkle of Christmas brings joy all year long. At the same time, I delight in decorating with the colors of a summer day.

I use color to define the architecture of a space, to connect one room to another, and to lead a client or hotel guest down a corridor or through a lobby. I use it in fabrics, carpets, draperies, and accessories to add glamour and vibrancy to a room. Although I have painted many projects in one dominant hue, such as red or black, I usually mix a variety of colors to create an exuberant mood. I use eight colors in almost every project, where appropriate: red, black, yellow, green, purple, pink, blue, and sky blue. These colors are my starting point, the palette I keep in mind as I begin. My neutral colors have never been cream, beige, or gray; they are soft Thomas Jefferson blue, sunshine yellow, cosmos pink, melon, and minty greens. Then, as if I am looking through a kaleidoscope, I give a traditional, elegant point of view a colorful twist.

My parents were avid gardeners, and so I grew up with an extensive knowledge of flowers as well as the belief that people who plant them are passionate about the future. Today, I keep a small balcony garden outside my New York City office for inspiration. When I create floral prints, I bring all the colors of the garden together, using, for example, tall purple hollyhocks as the background on draperies and tiny white sweet William for the border on an upholstered chair.

I tailor my color decisions to my clients' lifestyles, and my designs are inspired by the things they love. Charlene Nederlander, the wife of Broadway entrepreneur James Nederlander, and I have worked on seven residences together: one in Arizona, two in New York City, one in Southampton, and three in Palm Beach. Charlene loves color and wears it well. She is a collector of beautiful, wearable gemstones, and these jewels influence her choices at home.

One of my lifetime works has been the Greenbrier in West Virginia, which I have been decorating since the 1960s. Now, as the hotel's curator, I supervise all of the interior design work, from the new Casino Club that opened in 2010 to the PGA Classic event pavilions to the interiors of the soon-to-be Green-brier Presidential Express luxury train, which will travel from Washington, D.C. to White Sulphur Springs.

The job of decorating is never done. There is always something to update, restore, or refresh. And I am still at it—living a lifetime of colorful interior design and enjoying every single minute.

CARLETON VARNEY, 2011

Red

A room in red is like a lady in red: alluring and very appealing. I always recommend a red tie or carnation on a white sports coat for the gentleman who wants to attract attention. Red is also the color of Christmas when combined with fir-tree green. Red is the color of Valentine's Day, accompanied by candy pink and icing white. Some see red as the color of danger. Sailors take warning from a red sky in the morning. But I see red as the color of celebration. Whatever the associations, it brings excitement to any space.

I recently designed an apartment at the Ritz Carlton in Dallas, Texas, and painted every wall red. Hollywood glamour and nods to the West are everywhere in this bachelor pad, including a print of Slim Aarons' iconic photograph of the kings of the silver screen (Clark Gable, Van Heflin, Gary Cooper, and Jimmy Stewart), as well as a Remington bronze cowboy seated atop a console table in the living room. Raffia with accents of chocolate brown and metallic gold add to the mix.

CARLETON'S WORLD OF
Black

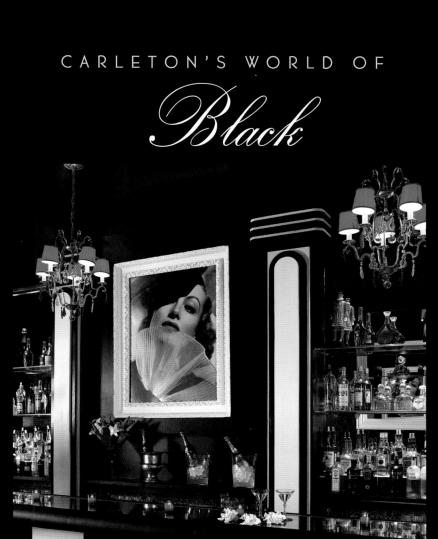

Dorothy Draper once said, "Every room needs a touch of black, perhaps in a vase, a lamp, a Chinese coffee table, or a leather blotter on the top of a desk in the library." I use black in interiors often. In fact, the walls in our curator's office at the Greenbrier are painted black lacquer above a crisp white wainscot. When presenting fabrics and decorative schemes to clients, I show colors and prints against a black backdrop to make them pop. And when my nephew, Josh Boyd, and his business partner, Darren Rubell, were opening a nightclub called Ella in New York, they came to me for the interior design. Black with white and dashes of red was my suggestion, and they followed through with the plan. I even painted the exterior of the club ebony black with white window trim and white door moldings.

Black is a mystery color, and black interiors are often the most dramatic. Black patent fabrics are reflective and can be used on upholstered furnishings, from very traditional to very contemporary.

Yellow

Yellow represents happiness, freedom, and, yes, memories—"tie a yellow ribbon round the old oak tree." Think sunshine and fields of late-summer corn. A yellow headboard, ceiling color, and even a lamp shade open a room to rays of sun when they cast their warm glow. I always say, "Happy colors make a happy home."

The logo for the Grand Hotel on Michigan's Mackinac Island features a bright-red horse-and-carriage motif on a sunny-yellow ground, welcoming guests as they arrive. The Jacqueline Kennedy Suite at the hotel has walls covered in a yellow stripe, with curtains and bed coverings to match. The carpet in the suite features the American Eagle in golds and yellows on a royal-blue ground.

The shelving in Fizzy's Land of Oz, the toy store at the Greenbrier, is painted yellow, which highlights the toys throughout the shop.

CARLETON'S WORLD OF
Green

Green is my favorite color. I like to paint small rooms with deep colors, such as midnight blue, garnet red, brown, or forest green, to make them cozy. The library in my home in County Limerick, Ireland, is painted a rich racing green, and I carpeted the floor in a red, green, black, and gold Tartan plaid. Dark-green walls were popular in the 1940s, when Modernists designed furniture in blond tones. The same rule applies to people: blonds look great in green and so do redheads. You could say that Irish ladies from the Emerald Isle, such as iconic screen actress Maureen O'Hara, give the color combination a very positive public image.

I use green-and-white-striped fabrics for awnings and upholstery, and I've used green-and-white-striped wallpaper in many rooms. It's one of my signature style elements.

Purple

Purple with red is a royal combination—very Buckingham Palace, which I experienced when I dined there. During the Carter Administration, I was asked by the White House Social Secretary, Gretchen Poston, to plan the décor of the State Dining Room for Margaret Thatcher's reception and dinner. I immediately chose lavenders, purples, and golds for the color scheme. The purple tablecloths were made from a quilted fabric, as were the dinner napkins, and all the linens were trimmed in red. Anemones in purple, red, and white were arranged in gold vermeil containers and precisely placed as centerpieces.

The Greenbrier has now been restored in original Dorothy Draper wallpapers and fabrics, including a lavender, purple, and pink Rhododendron print in the hallways. There simply is no color as romantic as lavender-pink. I use the warmth of lavender in sheeting designs as well as for table mats and napery.

CARLETON'S WORLD OF
Sky Blue

This blue is the color of the happiest sky, the Caribbean Sea, the ceilings on the porches at Thomas Jefferson's Monticello, and the gem stones aquamarine and larimar. It is a color my firm uses in its decorating work throughout the world for drapery fabrics, wall coverings, and furniture. I painted the interior of the small bowling alley at the Grand Hotel's Woods restaurant in mostly neutral tones, using a soft blue that has a touch of green to give it an aquamarine light.

The walls in my bedroom in New York City are painted heavenly blue to serve as the perfect background for my sky-blue-and-white-striped curtains. I love sleeping under a blue sky. Sky blue is also an excellent background choice for reds, browns, yellows, golds, pinks, and, of course, palm- and fir-tree greens. Nature always provides us with the colors that are universal, in both design and the world around us.

Pink

Enchanting pink is the most personal of all colors. Pink offers a delicate softness and changes the mood of absolutely anyone who enters a room, even from outright hostility to kindness.

Every skin tone is enhanced by pink. Just think of all the different shades offered at cosmetic counters. Touches of pink flowers in a vase or in a wallpaper pattern add the right note, inviting guests to stop and rest awhile. I often use a design called Princess Grace Rose in bedrooms. The wall covering was created for the room at the Greenbrier occupied by the late Princess of Monaco.

Pink can be used occasionally, on the back and side walls of a vitrine object case, or in other prominent ways, such as on the walls of a living room. Against pink, finer and bolder furnishings appear more subtle. For my friend and client Francie Whittenburg's villa on the island of St. Croix in the Caribbean, I combined pink with flamboyant orange in her dressing room to echo the tropical flowers outside.

CARLETON'S WORLD OF
Blue

Blues of every hue hold our dreams, soothe our souls, and provide our homes with tranquility. Dramatic blues with white have been immortalized in the porcelain and fabrics of many cultures. The Chinese have their blue-and-white Canton ware; the Spanish have their Azulejos tiles; the Danes have their Royal Copenhagen; and the French have their blue-and-white toiles. I love the blue found in many nautical designs, and fabrics with fish or rope patterns in blue and white always find special places in my decorating work. In fact, in my Palm Beach apartment, the walls throughout the condominium are painted rich skipper blue with white trim—a sharp contrast. I also show collectibles against blue and white and I often paint furniture white and accent the pieces with a blue trim for a touch of elegance. Painting old pieces of furniture white and adding a colorful trim can be quite effortless and have a brightening effect on a room.

Dear Dorothy,
 I know you are
watching over me from
above. I remember when I
first visited the Greenbrier
with you in the 1960s,
and my journey with
decorating began. Your
colors were special;
only you could put them
together in a sparkling
way. You inspired
me when you said,
"Decorators are born, not
made," and your words
of wisdom are always
with me. I shall continue
carrying on the tradition
of the gracious style that
you first created, and
which will never fade.
You are the best.
 With much admiration,
 Carleton

Memory for Color

The Greenbrier

During my early days with Dorothy Draper and Company, Inc., I attended a cocktail party for Prince Rainier and Princess Grace held in the President's Parlor at the Greenbrier. It was one of the many memorable events I was fortunate enough to be a part of, all because of Dorothy. When Dorothy first decorated the room, she painted it mint green. In keeping with her love of color while at the same time refreshing the palette, I turned the walls cantaloupe melon, which is flattering at night and glows during the day. My goal for the Greenbrier renovation overall was a simple one: to bring Dorothy's vision into the twenty-first century.

The wall color also provides the perfect contrast to the Delft-blue damask draperies that frame the French doors. Outside, a terrace overlooks the Allegheny Mountains.

In the President's Parlor, a landscape painting was made into two paintings, one for each side of the fireplace mantel. Dorothy chose to cut the canvas in half to provide the room with trees and a flowing river on both walls.

The wing chairs by the fireplace are covered in a Delft-blue damask drapery fabric, while the melon silk damask on two channel-back lounge chairs, called Delphine, coordinates with the wall color.

THIS PAGE:
The multifold, double-sided Coromandel screen has been in the President's Parlor since the early 1950s. The kidney-shaped sofa is a Kindel Furniture reproduction of a Dorothy Draper design for the restaurant that was known as the "Dorotheum" at the Metropolitan Museum of Art in New York.

OPPOSITE:
I commissioned the portrait of Princess Grace by Ralph Wolfe Cowan. It was Prince Rainier's favorite portrait of Grace, and there are only two in existence: one at the Greenbrier and the other in the Royal Palace in Monaco.

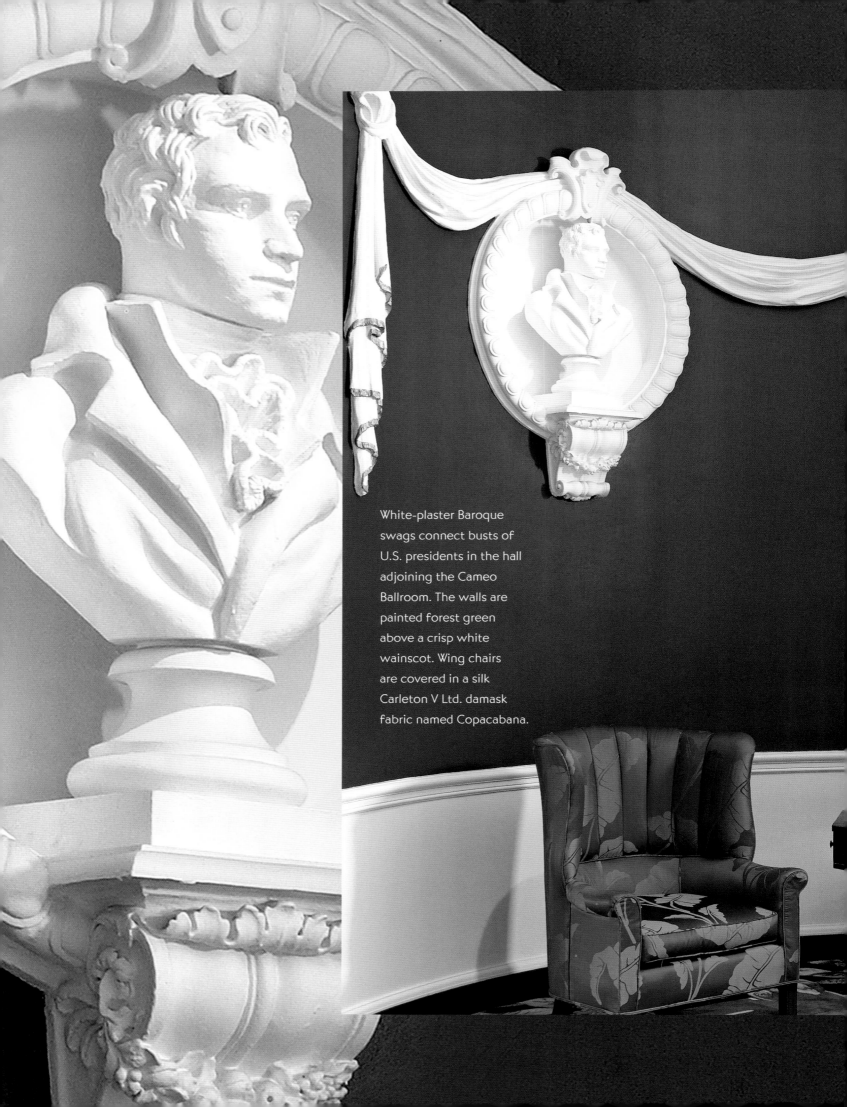

White-plaster Baroque swags connect busts of U.S. presidents in the hall adjoining the Cameo Ballroom. The walls are painted forest green above a crisp white wainscot. Wing chairs are covered in a silk Carleton V Ltd. damask fabric named Copacabana.

The Casino Club, with architecture by Michael Oliver McClung, includes three restaurants, a shopping concourse, and gaming rooms. The entry foyer combines all the colors I love with a traditional black-and-white checkerboard floor pattern in marble. The eighteen-inch squares are laid out on the diagonal—a Dorothy Draper design must. The columns are covered in a cerulean-blue-and-white-striped wallpaper, while Brazilliance, a pattern of green banana and grape leaves on a white ground, plays along the main walls. I like to think of accessories and special antique pieces as the "jewelry" in a space. In this hallway, the gold acanthus-leaf detail on the black-lacquer credenza and the brass railings on the stairs leading up to the hotel's reception lobby add a glittering touch.

OVERLEAF LEFT:
An eye-catching antique corner settee is placed for waiting guests outside Draper's Café. The unique piece is painted with white lacquer trimmed in gold leaf.

OVERLEAF RIGHT:
One of the white-plaster monkey wall sconces frolics happily on the banana- and grape-leaf wall covering.

The famous Brazilliance wall covering adds drama and color.

Dorothy's portrait is right at home in one of the Greenbrier's new casino restaurants, Draper's Café. The color scheme is inspired by Mrs. Draper's apartment at the Carlyle Hotel in New York, where she lived for more than thirty years. The walls are aubergine, a black-purple, and the banquettes are covered in one of Dorothy's favorite prints: bright-red roses intertwined with green leaves. The carpet is a vivid scarlet with a scattering of pink cabbage roses. The wall sconces are white plaster, and the white armchairs have cut-out backs and pink Naugahyde seats.

ABOVE:

The hand-painted mural by Alice Bear Ludwig in the French window depicts a view of the Springhouse at the resort.

THIS PAGE:
Oversized red and pink roses at the entrance of the Casino Club were painted on canvas that was stretched on the walls surrounding the double staircase.

OPPOSITE:
The Baroque shell-shaped water fountain is seen through the columns of a recreated Spring-house, on the main floor of the casino. Three exceptional chandeliers are installed above: the first one is a Marie-Thérèse—style fixture with aquamarine-blue crystals; the second was found in an antiques bazaar and comes from the original Euclid Avenue Fox Theater in Cleveland, Ohio; and the third, an American Vintage waterfall chandelier, hangs over the shell.

Lighting effects change the color of the water fountain, creating a dramatic entrance to the Casino Club. The etched-glass panel dividing one area of the casino from another also changes color.

I like bright colors,

bold contrasts, and floral patterns.

Large canvas wall-
covering panels from
Carleton V Ltd. of
scarlet-red, gold, white,
and silver tassels with
pineapple tops are
mounted high above
the gaming rooms.
I used the tassel as a
decorative element
throughout the casino.

THESE PAGES:
The Twelve Oaks
Lounge at the Casino
Club is named for the
famous plantation in
Margaret Mitchell's
novel, *Gone with the
Wind*. I placed oversized
blue-and-white-
porcelain Oriental
temple jars in front
of white Georgian
columns that have gold-
and-white pediments.
The wool carpet in
front of the bar was
custom-designed by
Brinsley Matthews and
fabricated by Ulster
Carpets of Ireland.

THESE PAGES:
Racing fans and the horsey
set love spending time in the
Twelve Oaks Lounge. The
Greenbrier partners with
Keeneland, a thoroughbred
racecourse in Kentucky, on
special events at the hotel.
The equestrian paintings
were commissioned from
Michael Christie, the resort's
artist in residence.

OVERLEAF LEFT:
The High Roller's Club in
the casino has a big-game
African-safari theme.
Honey-tone-finished wood
moldings with wall panels
upholstered in a tiger-stripe
print are essential
ingredients of the plan.
The chairs at the gaming
tables sport a woven fabric
of large green-and-brown
palm trees on a black
background, while the
wing chairs are covered
in a smaller-scale palm-
tree design.

OVERLEAF RIGHT:
Even the upholstery on
the bar stools—colorful
chessmen on a gold-and-
white checkerboard
pattern—continues the
game motif at the High
Roller's Club.

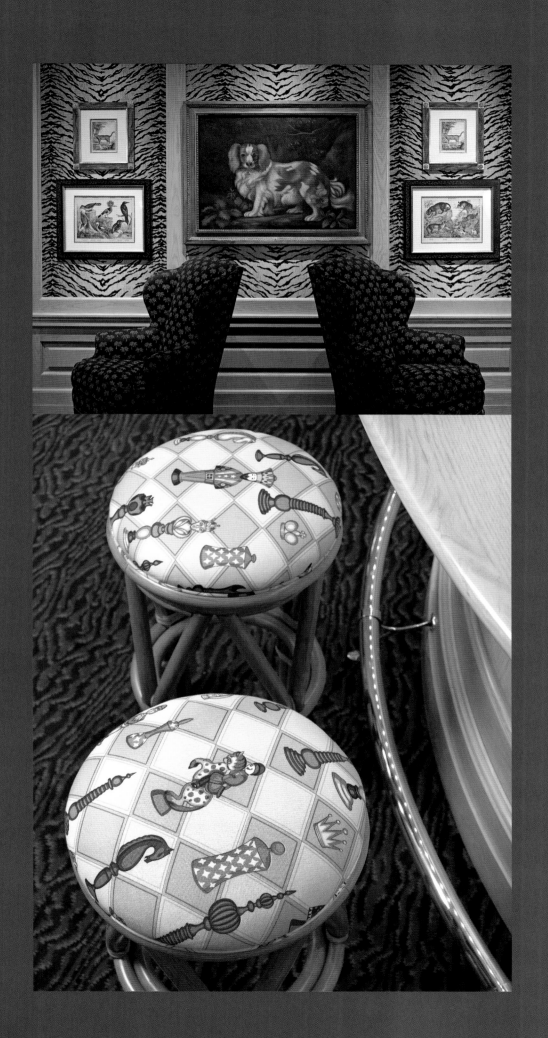

Every continent is represented in both the decoration and the cuisine served at the Greenbrier. A pair of happy dragons greets guests at the entry of Infusion, the Asian restaurant in the casino. The color scheme of the room is natural rattan with spicy paprika and sage green, along with Coromandel black for table linens and staff jackets.

ABOVE:
Antique Chinese tea canisters were collected from various sources from around the country and placed on wall-bracket shelving for a classic display.

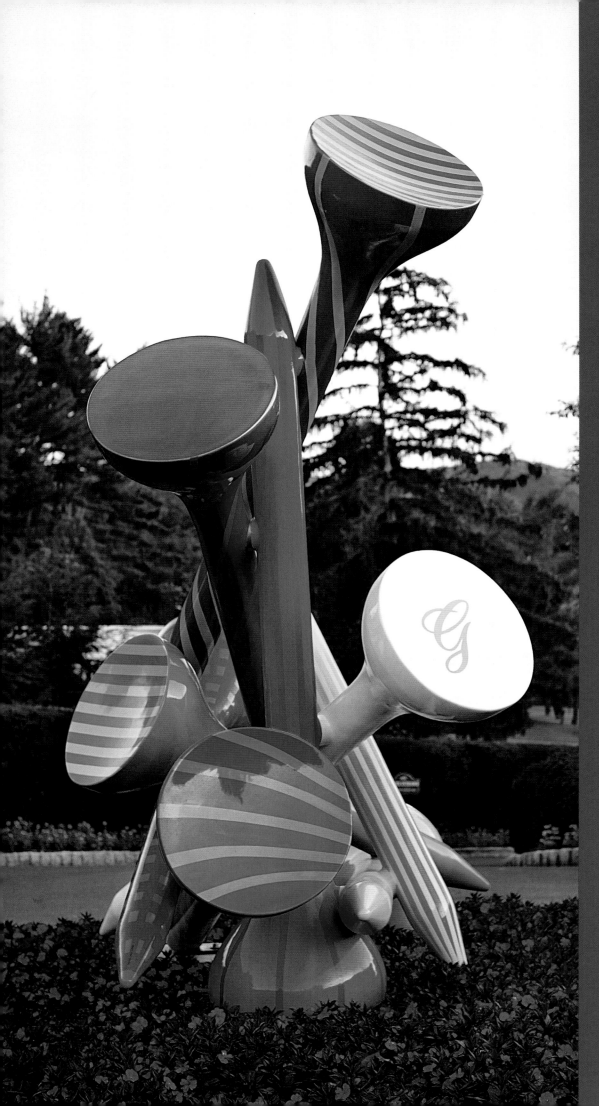

PREVIOUS PAGES:
The Greek Revival front entrance of the main building was renovated in 1930. Over the years, extensions were added to the original structure. Today the resort has 682 guest rooms. The Casino Club was built under the exterior front garden and pathways. The property, once owned by CSX Corporation (formerly the Chesapeake and Ohio Railway), was purchased by West Virginia–native Jim Justice and his family in 2009.

THESE PAGES:
One of the most exciting projects of my career has been creating the look for the new Greenbrier Classic, held annually in July in conjunction with the PGA Tour. I decided that all of the event pavilions should have green-and-white-striped awnings. Dorothy Draper's famous Rhododendron fabric covers the interior walls of the pavilions, mirroring the wallpaper in the guest-room corridors of the hotel. The "Tee" sculpture by artist Dan Meyer is positioned in beds of pink impatiens at the entrance to the golf-course clubhouse.

OVERLEAF:
The resort boasts four spectacular championship golf courses, including the famous Old White. My friend and legendary golfer, the late Sam Snead, was once Golf Professional Emeritus at the Greenbrier. Today, Tom Watson, another great player, holds this prestigious title.

FORUM
WINE BAR AND PIZZERIA

THESE PAGES AND PREVIOUS PAGES:
The Greenbrier goes all the way to bring its guests the cuisines of the world. The new Forum restaurant inside the main hotel was designed and decorated by yours truly. The ceramic-tile bar front, the colorful striped ceiling, a blue-and-white gingham-check fabric, and a photographic scenic backdrop were inspired by Italian visual delights, from Roma to Venezia to Firenzi.

New York City is a metropolis of concrete-and-steel high-rises, yet there are neighborhoods where the townhouse life that we associate with the grace and elegance of days gone by still exists. Luckily, today many of these buildings are protected as landmarks. Downtown in the West Village and uptown along Fifth Avenue, there are charming houses with inviting front doors and small back gardens where flowers and trees grow.

My clients Nancy Abraham and Arnold Moss lived in an apartment in a skyscraper before purchasing a New York townhouse with quite a history. The actress Tallulah Bankhead once lived here, as did the author Tom Wolfe and the Academy Award–winning actress Julie Andrews.

Nancy and Arnold are well traveled, humanitarians, and animal lovers—all of which mirror qualities that are easy to bring into the home with color: sophistication, warmth, and fun! The three of us put our heads together to renovate the house completely.

Town

house
Color

Uptown Style

The back garden of Nancy Abraham's and Arnold Moss's Upper East Side residence stays colorful and cool ten months out of the year, thanks to its beautiful green foliage. French doors on the extension, along with skylights above, provide sunshine to the house.

Their home has many features typical of a townhouse: a single-family, three-story structure sharing a common wall with neighbors, natural light sources in both the front and back, and an entrance on street level.

My idea was to bring as much of the garden's natural color themes inside as possible.

We decided to create an attractive entrance on the ground floor. Stepping into the foyer, with its stenciled-wood floor (checkerboard blond and walnut squares), you are greeted by Nancy and Arnold's extensive collection of books, which reflects their many and varied interests, including travel to faraway places, art, and antiques. I painted the wall behind the bookcases a fresh mint green to contrast with the darker colors of the spines and set off other treasures, such as Staffordshire dog figurines. The English pen armchairs are upholstered in my favorite plaid check of melon, green, gold, and red, and match the simple roman shade. I repeated these same colors throughout the house.

ABOVE:

Nancy's heart boxes are arranged on an inlaid-marble table. For me, a black-and-white checkerboard pattern—in any size and material—works in every room, in every project, big or small.

PREVIOUS PAGES:

The family room is on the ground floor, off the kitchen. Instead of installing wallpaper, the walls were stenciled with a pattern in gold over russet. The armchair next to the fireplace is covered in an animal print on a background that matches the wall color, while an antique, Edwardian-style tufted chair is upholstered in a black horsehair fabric. Not all of the furniture in a room has to share the same upholstery. Difference adds depth.

THESE PAGES:

On the second floor, the drawing room overlooks the garden. To enhance the green from outside, I paired green with red in the room—a classic color combination. Mixing a rich, Venetian-red wall color with apple-green drapery and pale-lavender furniture is not all that complicated if you are a lover of color and willing to take the plunge. I organized several seating areas in the room, combining a variety of fabrics, from silk satins to velvets, as well as different furniture styles. I always spend time creating drapery treatments, especially valances. I designed the three here to look as though they were handcrafted by a seamstress at a haute-couture fashion house.

ABOVE:

Different floral patterns can work together to great effect, as shown by this pairing of a floral black-lacquer chest and silk-upholstered club chair.

RIGHT:

A landscape painting by the master French Impressionist Alfred Sisley hangs over the white Greek Revival fireplace in the drawing room. The wing chair is upholstered in a striped lavender and soft-green velvet fabric.

OPPOSITE:

Window treatments are what decorating is all about. Valances with bowties, rosettes, red fringe, and braids are some of the details that add sophistication to the room.

Arnold Moss enjoys having his library and office in the front of the house. Black pin-striped fabric covers the walls and serves as background to a superb collection of oil paintings of dogs. The upholstery in the room mixes a scenic print on the sofa with red crewelwork on the cream armchair.

OVERLEAF LEFT:
One of a pair of Biedermeier side tables, with its warm tone and gold-trimmed dragon stand, echoes the gilded picture frames on the wall.

OVERLEAF RIGHT:
The ceiling of the library has been covered in gold foil and brushed with red paint. The glow from an Italian chandelier with sculptured glass flames reflects off the metallic surface to warm the room.

THIS PAGE:
Nancy and Arnold love the violets in their bedroom: on the carpet, on the drapery and upholstery, and on the bed linens. The wallpaper mimics a white cane motif over a lavender ground, a pattern I created named Cane.

OPPOSITE:
The chandelier, a Murano glass piece made in Italy and designed especially for the residence, also has a hint of lavender.

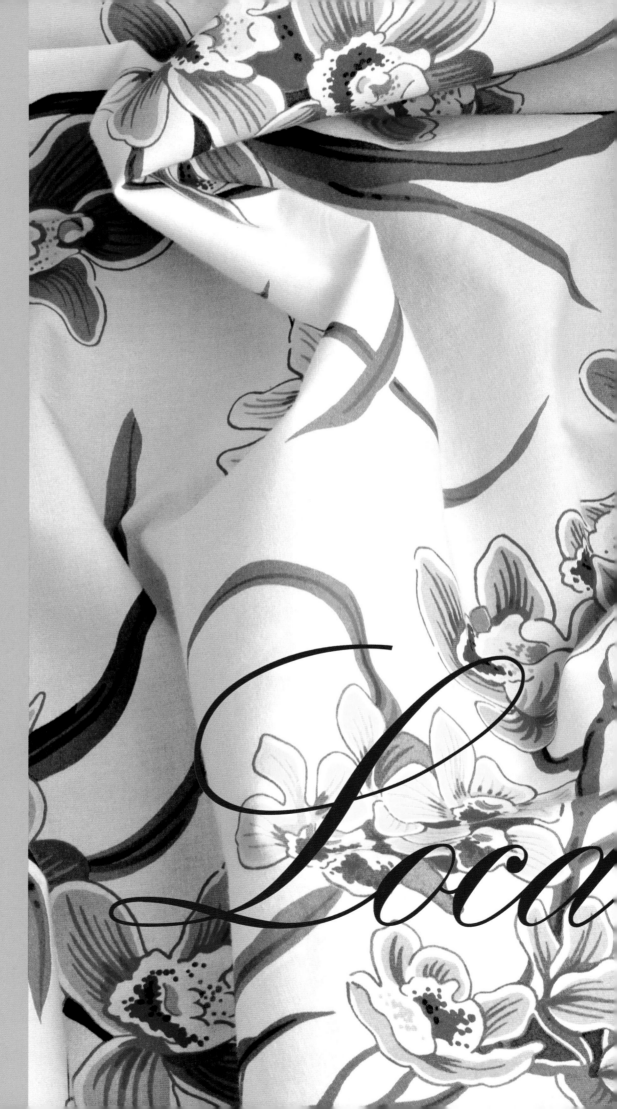

Florida has been a part of my life since I started designing interiors in 1964. I've decorated hotels on the east coast, west coast, and in the midlands, as well as residences from Tampa to Jacksonville and Vero Beach to Palm Beach.

Florida has many blues and greens. If you believe that palm trees grow statewide, you haven't visited Jacksonville, where pine trees dominate the terrain. The colors of Florida are not the colors of the Caribbean. They are the soft, old, weathered-wood shingle kind: pineapple, lime, lemon, pale blue, pink, and cantaloupe melon. The light is also not as powerful. I always paint a color sample on a wall and then stand back to check the hue. Usually, the color I expect is not the color I get.

Loca

At Home in Palm Beach

I bought this three-bedroom villa two years ago, and though it isn't my first home in Palm Beach, it is the latest. Built in the 1950s, these properties were the first low-rise condominiums in the area.

Inside, I chose a nautical-blue color scheme to unify the decoration. I find that one color used throughout a space makes for a larger look. This was my first all-blue environment: blue sky, blue water, blue rooms.

A full-size department-store mannequin of one of my favorite silver-screen stars, Betty Grable, stands in the corner of the living room near the kitchen-counter bar. Behind "Betty" is a painting by Sir Paul McCartney, titled *Bull*.

THIS PAGE:

Palm Beach is an island: on one side is
the Atlantic Ocean and on the other is
Florida's Intracoastal Waterway. The
blue sky and waving palm trees
are inspirational to me;
many rooms in my work
have ceilings that
are painted soft
blue, sometimes
even with white
puffy clouds. The green
color of palm fronds has been
represented in fabrics and wall
coverings I have designed for
projects from the Caribbean and south
Florida to the Hawaiian Islands.

OPPOSITE:

The property is surrounded by the Sunshine
State's lush natural flora. Bougainvillea
covers the arched entryway of the
residence. In this picture, the branches
have just been trimmed of their
blossoms, leaving a lone bloom
swimming in vibrant green.

The main living space includes sliding doors onto a dining terrace that overlooks the Intracoastal Waterway. A wall-size mirror opens up the room and a large curved sectional sofa in white linen faces the water views. The painted-white coffee table is a Dorothy Draper design. Some of the pillows and the club chair are covered in a red-on-white Carleton Varney By the Yard™ fabric called Big Fish. The design is available in many colors, and I thought it would be fun to mix red, white, and blue for this color scheme.

OVERLEAF:

This narrow fruitwood cabinet was once one of a pair used in a library for displaying books. I painted it white, white, white— very Elsie de Wolfe, and Dorothy Draper too, of course. It adds a period look to the otherwise modern apartment. The cabinet holds my pride and joy: a collection of Flora Danica dinnerware from Royal Copenhagen, the centuries-old Danish porcelain manufacturer for whom I designed china in the mid 1970s. The pattern dates back to the company's eighteenth-century origins and reportedly was a gift from the King of Denmark to Catherine the Great of Russia.

THIS PAGE:

The pagoda-top curio cabinet is from my collection for Kindel Furniture. Dorothy Draper originally designed the Chinoiserie piece for the Greenbrier. (Her version sits in the Peacock Lobby area off the hotel's main dining room.) I painted the interior wall Chinese red to coordinate with the coral-shaped wall sconces. The floor is covered in glazed-ceramic Mexican tile, which stays cool in the Florida heat. The tiles are another unifying element used throughout the house.

OPPOSITE:

I found the obelisk-shaped étagère shelf in a department store in Washington, D.C. It holds a few of my special treasures: a white Staffordshire dog, a favorite accessory throughout many of my projects; a photograph of me with my son Sebastian; an Irish toby jug for good luck; and a glass head statue. One of a pair of Zebra-print armless chairs from Kindel flanks the unit. I love the contrast of light furniture against a dark wall color.

Good morning, Sunshine! Since I am from the North (I was born in Lynn, Massachusetts), I come to Florida seeking the sun. I painted the ceiling of my Palm Beach bedroom sunshine yellow so I can lie in bed and look up at the brightness! The walls are painted with five-inch-wide nautical-blue and white vertical stripes. Contemporary wall shelves hung over the bed hold blue- and clear-glass flying fish.

The arched headboard is covered in lemon-yellow moiré to match the club chair and ottoman. Moiré adds a glamorous texture to the room. The bed linens are reversible, providing the opportunity to have either a masculine look with the big blocks of color or a more feminine version with the floral pattern. The mirror surround is made of white plaster, as are the palm-tree and pineapple lamps that sit upon Dorothy Draper night tables.

OPPOSITE:

Several years ago, I designed reading glasses in every shade and called them Carleton Varney's Eye Candy™. Now they are part of my own colorful accessories and I keep them handy for reading in bed. I picked up the pineapple lamp at a garage sale in Port Antonio, Jamaica. Made of wood, the base is painted in its original yellow and green; I added the white-linen shade.

CARLETON VAR

La Coquille

Richard Roberts came across one of my
books just when he and his wife, Sandy,
were considering the renovation of their
three-bedroom condominium at the
La Coquille Villas in Manalapan, Florida,
near Palm Beach. I am inspired by the
region's natural surroundings, especially
the ocean. I like to create an interior as
a musician writes a symphony, always
repeating the melody, and in this case the
melody was color: aquamarine.

Bamboo trees grow throughout
the area. I first saw bamboo used as an
architectural element in Polynesia, where
I designed hotels in the 1960s and 1970s.
I brought them into the design for the
Roberts' apartment.

PREVIOUS PAGES:

In the Roberts' entryway, I covered one wall with trompe l'oeil louvered-shutter wallpaper to create an open, outdoor look. A full-length mirror on the opposite wall reflects the design and gives a larger spatial feel. I painted aquamarine-blue and white stripes on the ceiling and used Caribbean-blue glazed ceramic tiles in the foyer and connecting living room. I traveled to the tile manufacturer in Tlaquepaque, Mexico, and worked with the craftsmen there to paint them in the exact shade I wanted.

THESE PAGES:

I love to combine stripes, prints, and plaids, and I did just that in the living room. Have you ever seen a plaid in pink, aqua, and green on a white-linen ground? Probably not! Plaids are usually associated with Scotland and darker colors. I had the plaid for the Roberts' home specially woven in Mexico to coordinate with the solid fabrics in the room. The sofa is upholstered in an aquamarine chenille fabric and the throw pillows are covered with Cymbidium Orchid, one of my designs. The lavender-pinks and whites of the tropical flower are entwined with green leaves on a soft-pink background.

The ceiling fan is shaped in a modern design and hangs from a circular recess, which I painted with stripes for a tented effect.

OPPOSITE:

Oh, Dorothy, how you have influenced my life and decorating career! I adapted this sparkling-white chest, known as the Brazilliance commode, from an original design Mrs. Draper created for the Quitandinha Hotel in Petropolis, Brazil. It features Dorothy's Baroque feathered scrolls on each side, but is slightly smaller than its predecessor to make it a perfect fit for the Roberts' bedroom. Inside the cabinet are drawer shelves and on top sit two antique blue-and-speckled-gold Murano glass lamps from Italy. The Regency mirror is a find from a London antique shop. The crown molding in this room, and throughout the apartment, is natural bamboo, faux-finished in a blond hue to hide any irregular joining.

THIS PAGE:

When shopping in Mexico for the ocean-side villa, I discovered a tile pattern that reminded me of a kaleidoscope. It was hand painted in white, deep Caribbean blue, and sand. Naturally, being me, I wanted to include hibiscus pink in the overall scheme, so I picked a flower from the hibiscus plant just outside the Roberts' window and used it to inspire the linen fabric for the bedroom club chair.

The Grand Hotel has been the reigning Queen of the Great Lakes for many years, and host to presidents, royalty, sports luminaries, and movie stars for more than a century. It is color magic in every way—in the design of the lobby carpeting, wallpapers, needlepoint upholstery, and wall color of the guest facilities. Bright geranium red is prominent throughout the hotel, a six-star resort on an island with no cars.

The ceilings at the Grand Hotel are Thomas Jefferson blue, and the columns on the front porch are white white—just like all the mansions of the world. There are suites individually decorated in all the colors I like best, from the Jacqueline Kennedy Suite to the Jefferson Suite to the latest Lilac Suite. Pink, blue, orange, lavender, emerald, garnet—the colors of the rainbow, and somewhere over the rainbow—are brought together in this property. The hotel's owners, Dan and Amelia Musser, handed me a blank canvas in 1976, and I have enjoyed painting it ever since.

The Grand Hotel

A summer resort from an era gone by, the Grand Hotel was built before air conditioning, when families sought out a cooler place to spend May through September. It boasts the largest porch in the world—all furnished with white rocking chairs, which I put in place with the blessings of the hotel's owners. The awnings are yellow-gold with green and white underside stripes, and the American flags are ceremonially raised and lowered each day.

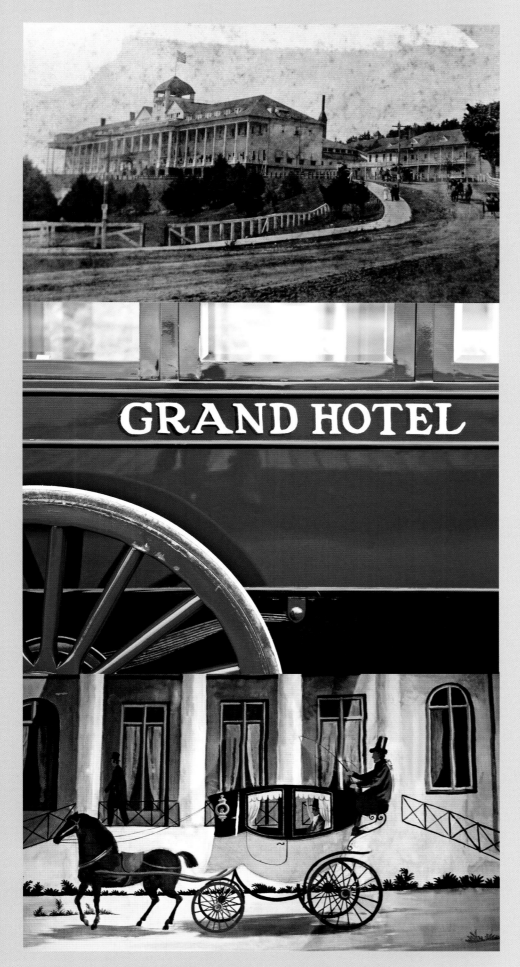

What was best yesterday is classic today and therefore the design style of the future.

PREVIOUS PAGES:

It's bicycle or horse-drawn carriage for everyone who gets off the boat at Mackinac Island. You take a step back in time when you come for a visit. The uniforms of the carriage drivers were designed with a wink to the past: white britches, a red jacket with gold buttons, an Abe Lincoln top hat, and shiny black patent-leather riding boots.

THESE PAGES:

The Grand Hotel has always been in style for its dignity, spirit, graciousness, and color. May we never lose the elements of glamour and comfort that the resort offers, including the royal-red carpet that is always rolled out for guests.

THESE PAGES:
Geranium red says it all, in both the wing chairs and the Edwardian-style carpeting in the hotel lobby corridor: the geraniums are there to stay. The murals at either end of the lobby depict eighteenth-century life with its charming horse-drawn carriages.

OVERLEAF:
Mackinac means "turtle" in the language of the Ojibway tribe, the Native Americans who named this delightful island—located in the Straits of Mackinac between the United States and Canada—for its shape. I placed an impressive but faux turtle shell on a console table in the lobby.

OPPOSITE AND LEFT:
An antique Venetian mirror, accented with pink-glass flower adornments, hangs on an emerald-green wall in the lobby and reflects the schooner boat placed on the table in the foreground.

ABOVE:
Over the years, I have found interesting objects, vintage photographs, and artworks, such as this series of nineteenth-century etchings of presidential portraits, to install in the hallways and guest corridors of the hotel.

In the Geranium Bar, every table has a lakefront view. The geranium-red chairs have black needlepoint cushions with a geranium at the center. Hooray for green walls, an aqua-blue ceiling, and white-marble tabletops! This is just the right place to enjoy a fruit-filled beverage.

OPPOSITE:
A Dublin typeface was used for the dining-room sign set beneath the fan-shaped transom above the entry door. Sheet mirror has been installed on the columns, which run the length of the building and reflect light and glorious views of Lake Michigan from the large open windows. Green crystal-trimmed Hundai lanterns hang above the long red-and-green runner carpet in the central arcade between the dining rooms.

THIS PAGE:
Red geraniums grace the Salle à Manger in the porch's window boxes. The dining room chairs have backs in green and white stripes.

OVERLEAF:
This room is even longer than the ceremonial dining room at Buckingham Palace—where dining at the long table, set with countless flowers and epergnes filled with fresh fruit, is a once-in-a-lifetime experience. The Grand Hotel's main dining room is equally festive and lit by a parade of chandeliers in my marigold print: yellow and orange flowers intertwined with green leaves on a white background.

OPPOSITE AND TOP RIGHT:
When I started decorating
the dining room at the Grand
Hotel thirty-five years ago,
the walls were lemon yellow
to coordinate with the yellow
marigolds in the drapery and
lamp-shade fabric. In 2002, I
changed the color to frosted
orange sherbet to coordinate
with the orange marigolds in
the pattern.

Table lamps on the sides
of banquettes add an intimate
feel and residential look to
the dining room. The ban-
quettes are also upholstered
in my marigold fabric.

RIGHT:
The Dorothy Draper china
pattern was originally used
in the now-extinct Camellia
House at the Drake Hotel in
Chicago. Before I came to
the Grand Hotel, Mr. and Mrs.
Musser purchased the floral
tableware because they loved
its garden-inspired design.
I would never change it.

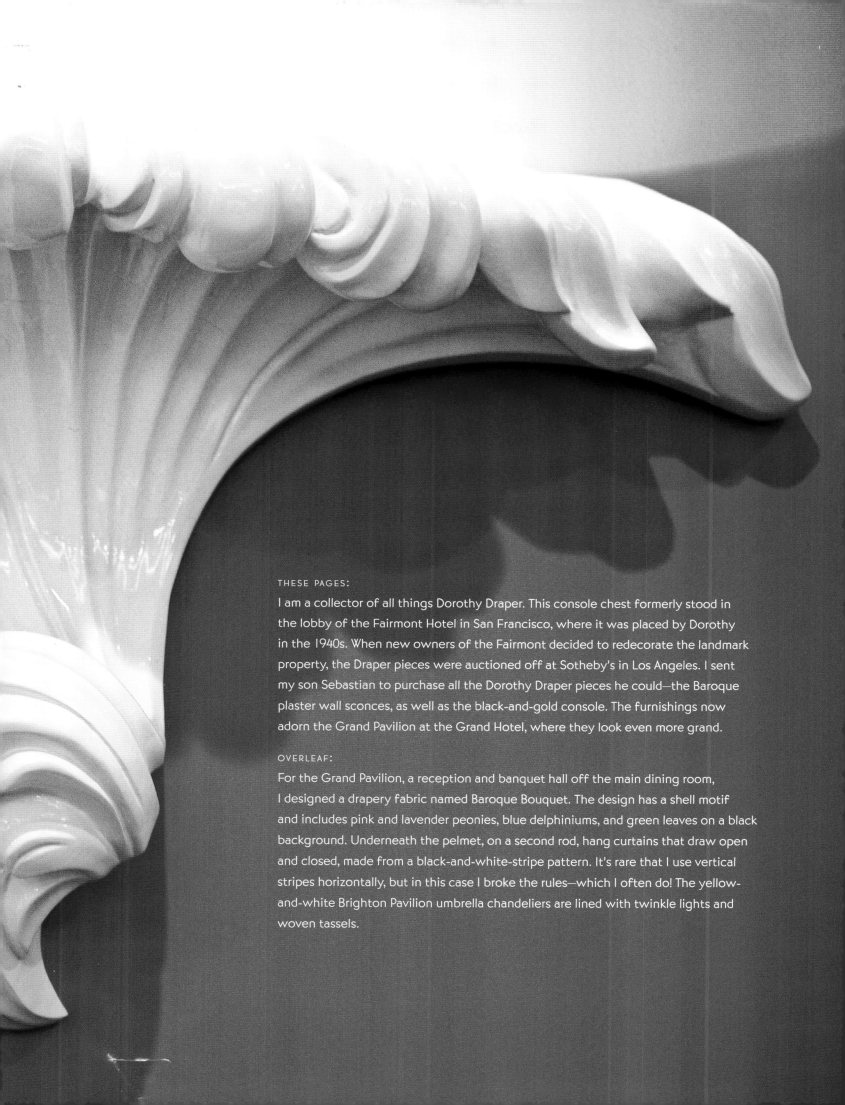

THESE PAGES:

I am a collector of all things Dorothy Draper. This console chest formerly stood in the lobby of the Fairmont Hotel in San Francisco, where it was placed by Dorothy in the 1940s. When new owners of the Fairmont decided to redecorate the landmark property, the Draper pieces were auctioned off at Sotheby's in Los Angeles. I sent my son Sebastian to purchase all the Dorothy Draper pieces he could—the Baroque plaster wall sconces, as well as the black-and-gold console. The furnishings now adorn the Grand Pavilion at the Grand Hotel, where they look even more grand.

OVERLEAF:

For the Grand Pavilion, a reception and banquet hall off the main dining room, I designed a drapery fabric named Baroque Bouquet. The design has a shell motif and includes pink and lavender peonies, blue delphiniums, and green leaves on a black background. Underneath the pelmet, on a second rod, hang curtains that draw open and closed, made from a black-and-white-stripe pattern. It's rare that I use vertical stripes horizontally, but in this case I broke the rules—which I often do! The yellow-and-white Brighton Pavilion umbrella chandeliers are lined with twinkle lights and woven tassels.

At the top of the hotel, there is a duplex cocktail lounge called the Cupola Bar. The space was originally a crow's nest, used by the early owners to watch cruise ships sail up and down the Great Lakes. I like to think of the room as my stairway-to-the-stars observatory. The royal-blue carpet on the stairs to the lounge is star studded.

RIGHT AND OPPOSITE:
Old maps of the Great Lakes hang on the flocked royal blue–on–blue-striped wall covering. Believe it or not, you can still find flocking machines to recreate the look of yesteryear. A glass chandelier made in Murano, Italy, brightens both rooms, upstairs and downstairs. Glass geraniums grace the branches of the elegant fixture.

The Grand Hotel has more than three-dozen named suites, with décor designed to realize each theme—or my fantasy version of it. For the Napoleon Suite, I used a burgundy-drapery wallpaper with a gold-tassel border as the baseboard molding. The room is filled with Napoleonic-era mirrors, etchings, and furniture. Napoleon would have been happy here—at least I think he would have been. The Josephine Suite adjoins his with connecting doors.

For the Josephine Suite, the Austrian Shade wall covering in aqua blues on white sets the mood. Carved fruitwood furnishings are everywhere—a bed, night tables, a vanity, dressers, and chairs. I bought the entire collection at a New York City flea market on a Sunday morning in July. For the upholstery on the bergères in the suite, I used my design Sweet Violets in lavender and purple on a white background. At the windows, Josephine gets the same glamorous lace treatment she would have worn for her dressing gown. The antique gold holdbacks are the details I call the jewelry in a room.

All the beds in the Grand Hotel are special, but the walnut-finished canopy bed in the Lord Astor Suite is exemplary in the details of the curtain fabric, especially the brown-and-off-white fringe tassels. The Astor family were once fur traders and lived on the island. To celebrate their connection to Mackinac history, we named and decorated two suites in honor of Lord and Lady Astor.

When I served as the
design consultant to
President and Mrs. Carter
at the White House
in the 1970s, I was
fascinated by the
Lincoln Bedroom. With
the Mussers' enthusiastic
approval, I created
a Lincoln Suite. The
pale-green walls, velvet
upholstery, and dark
mahogany closely
resemble the famous
room in Washington as
I remember it.

Details, details, details, in yellow, pink, and green, complete the Woodfill Suite. Stewart Woodfill was the bachelor uncle of Dan Musser. Uncle Woodfill, as I called him, was a David Niven–style man, ascot and velvet smoking jacket included, and his eccentricities were many. He was not in favor of changing any of the decorations at the Grand, not even a single chair in the lobby. He eventually let his nephew take charge of the challenge, and it was Dan and Amelia who engaged the services of my firm. In the end, after the completion of the lobby and dining-room designs, Uncle Woodfill beckoned me to his side, shook my hand, and said, "Great job, young man." Uncle Woodfill had only just begun to be "Draperized."

Mr. Color

The Hollywood Grand Suite

Of course, the Hollywood Grand Suite has a big star on the door. Many remember the 1932 film *Grand Hotel*, which was my inspiration for the deluxe décor. The room has signed photographs of such Hollywood actors and actresses as Lana Turner, Rita Hayworth, Van Johnson, Fred Astaire, Greta Garbo, and, of course, my client for many years, Joan Crawford.

THIS PAGE:

I used a color scheme of
hunter green, red, gold,
and blue for the Governor
Milliken Suite, named after
one of Michigan's favorite
leaders. The bed, with a
ruby-red canopy and
solid-brass fluted-tubing
posters, was custom-
made for the suite.

OPPOSITE:

The bed linens, draperies,
and upholstery are part
of a group of fabrics
I designed called the
Heraldry Collection.
The ornamental pattern
includes shields of
armor laced with ropes
of tassels and cording.

THESE PAGES:

Over the river and to Woods Restaurant we go! Several years ago, Dan and Amelia purchased the children's playhouse on the Mackinac Island Estate, a property once owned by Michael Cudahy, who made millions in the meatpacking business and had a mansion on the island. The structure, originally built for the seven Cudahy children, with a stage for rainy-day theatrical plays and a miniature bowling alley, was run down. I suggested turning the building into an alpine chalet in the style of Julie Andrews' *Sound of Music*. I painted the exterior the same forest green I used at the Grand Hotel, with bright-yellow and scarlet-red details on the window boxes and above the doors and windows.

OVERLEAF:

The main dining room, with its high vaulted ceilings, faux-antler chandeliers, red walls, and giant fireplaces, has a dramatic feeling.

Mackinac Magic

Dan and Amelia Musser came into my life in 1976, when they called me about redecorating the Grand Hotel. Amelia often refers to me as the Grand's ninetieth birthday present. The Mussers are not only my clients but also the best of friends. We've been through a lot of ups and downs together—all of them, I'd say, colorful.

Corner Cottage is the Mussers' Mackinac Island dwelling during the summer. The house has a white picket fence and a railing on the porch inspired by Thomas Jefferson's Monticello. I decided the exterior should be a soft morning-glory blue and the front door a welcoming sunshine yellow. "Just a home of morning glories that you read about in stories." So goes the song from the 1940s that my mother, Julia, would sing to me, and it was my inspiration for the Mussers' residence.

Antique carriage lanterns light the Mussers' front porch and door in the evenings. The rattan and white-wicker pieces, all from the hotel, continue the summer spirit of the legendary resort island. The seating cushions are in my green-and-white-striped awning fabric.

OVERLEAF:
In the Mussers' living room, the woodwork is painted white—beams and all. Staffordshire dogs sit on pedestals above the fireplace. A garland of white-painted flower reliefs decorates the mantel. The wing chairs are covered in aqua-blue and white stripes. The drapery fabric is called Tarkington Hall, one of the Carleton V Ltd. prints: pinks and aquas on a pale-gray ground.

The pagoda valances are edged in white brush fringe and furnished with small wooden bell tassels. My Staffordshire dogs go everywhere with me, as they do here in the Mussers' azalea-pink dining room. The eighteenth-century dining chairs are painted white, as is the ball-and-claw-footed dining table. A morning-glory design has been painted below the crown molding around the walls.

OPPOSITE:
To make the room shine, I placed silver pieces in an antique breakfront trimmed in morning-glory blue.

THIS PAGE:
The Mussers' unique
collection of antiques,
such as an heirloom rocker
from Amelia's family and
a blue-and-white plate
with an image of the
Grand Hotel in the center,
gives the house much
personal character.

OPPOSITE:
A Chinoiserie trellis frame
surrounds the entrance
to the upstairs bedrooms,
and an antique secretary
on the landing creates
a room out of an often-
ignored space.

OVERLEAF:
A Venetian mirror reflects
the bed in one of the guest
rooms in the Mussers' home,
where I always stay when
I am on the island. The
rose-and-trellis fabric is
a Carleton V Ltd. design.
I have used it for laminated
pull-down window shades,
the bedspread, and the
quilted headboard.

Lynette and Richard Merillat came to me for color. They had visited the Grand Hotel on Mackinac Island, which was near their home-to-be on Lake Charlevoix in northern Michigan. We met to talk about their dreams for the lake house, which was to become Lynette's fantasy home, one filled with color and her special antique furniture and decorative items. We shopped together and found pieces that completed Lynette's collections and made the house, well, not your ordinary lakeside retreat. Architect Andre Poineau has built several homes on the Michigan lakes, but this house—named White Pines for the trees on the property, and measuring 17,500 square feet with a 10,300-square-foot boathouse—is the finest project of his career because of its scale and sense of grandeur.

Color Inside

Out

By the Lake

The Merillats and I, along with Andre
Poineau, put our imaginations together
to design both the exterior and interior
details of their lake house, down to
the decorative hardware, wall color,
light fixtures, furniture, upholstery, and
artwork. Every last inch was taken into
account, including this arched entrance
to the triple garage—a fir-green door with
red trim and elegant ornamental handles.

Poineau is also a pilot, and he took photographer Michel Arnaud up in his Cessna to capture White Pines on Lake Charlevoix and the surrounding forest. When I presented the Merillats with the colors I had selected for the exterior of the house—a red roof and green shingles—they happily agreed. I've been told that boaters on the lake often cruise by very slowly to take in the never-before-seen color combination.

OVERLEAF:
With red and green as the predominant exterior coloring, the house makes a picture-perfect Christmas-card image when the roof is laden with snow.

Mr. Color

OPPOSITE:
Seen here from the upper balcony, the double-height drawing room has cosmos-pink walls, which serve as background to a welcoming mix of Victorian and Edwardian portraits, as well as an aqua-blue Dorothy Draper Brazilliance commode. The mirror above the carved-oak mantelpiece is from Syria, and the chandelier is made of wrought iron.

THIS PAGE:
The drawing room represents Carleton Varney color all the way: white-on-blue cane prints mixed with raspberry, white, and gold stripes, and floral patterns. The Merillats' existing furniture was used in the planning of the interiors so that everything came together to give the house the personality of its owners.

The stained-glass shade on the standing lamp in the drawing room tells the color story of the Merillats' interior: aqua, pink, pearlized white, and gold.

The drawing-room furniture grouping includes two sofas covered in a raspberry chenille and four swivel split-back lounge chairs from Kindel in a Rhododendron covering. I specially designed the carpet, a white cane-weave pattern on a Thomas Jefferson–blue background, for the residence, and it was woven by McMurray of Ireland. A family collection of crystal candlesticks sits on the ample coffee table.

A house without its owner's soul is not a home at all.

RIGHT:

My inspiration for the interior of the house was all the colors of a country garden gathered together in a bouquet.

BELOW:

Lynette Merillat has collected blue hobnail glass in all shapes and sizes for many years.

OPPOSITE:

The kitchen captures the fun-loving spirit of the house Lynette and Richard envisioned for themselves, their three daughters, and all their grandchildren, who adore visiting. The antique carousel horses prance on a ledge overlooking the room, set off by a wall painted in fifteen-inch-wide stripes for a Varney carnival-tent look.

PREVIOUS LEFT:

A table for two is placed in front of a fireplace in the kitchen. Wing chairs, covered in a fabric named Boca Grande, offer a living-room feel to the setting and make it a comfortable place for Lynette and Richard to enjoy an intimate at-home breakfast, lunch, or dinner when the rest of the family is not staying with them.

PREVIOUS RIGHT:

An oval-shaped table was custom-made for the kitchen dining area and gives a formal look to the room. The kidney-shaped sofas by Kindel are in loveseat dimensions, seating two, and are upholstered in the same Rhododendron fabric used on the club chairs in the adjoining drawing room.

TOP RIGHT AND OPPOSITE:

The dome-shaped, stained-glass ceiling is the focus of the kitchen. Its pattern features the trillium flower, one of the forest flowers indigenous to northern Michigan. The bronze and crystal chandelier is ornamented with glass garden flowers.

BOTTOM RIGHT:

A detail of this table base, revealing golden swans and acanthus leaves, suggests the waterside setting of the house.

Attention to detail is my trademark. This antique, once-derelict settee with matching chairs was reconditioned with aqua-blue chenille, chartreuse-green trim, and black six-inch-bullion fringe. I found the pieces in an Upstate New York antiques barn one summer weekend. I placed them in Mrs. Merillat's private den just off the drawing room, where we hung a painting of a little girl looking out the window.

OPPOSITE:
Glass finials on the stair posts are filled with flowers. The garden theme is conveyed throughout the house in many different materials.

TOP:
The gallery on the second-floor landing overlooks the drawing room and has a view of the lake. It is the ideal place to relax and take in the Merillats' painting collection.

LEFT:
A Victorian suite including loveseat and chairs was purchased at a Sotheby's auction and re-covered in a raspberry fabric from Carleton V Ltd.

OVERLEAF LEFT AND RIGHT:
Details such as welting, cord, nail heads, pediments, and even belt buckles that become artworks when hung on the grass-cloth walls in Richard's study, are important to the design of the room. Furniture from the Merillats' collection is covered in a gold chenille. I designed the carpet in an Indian style, and it was manufactured by Dixon Carpets in Connemara, Ireland.

RALPH LAUREN

ARTIST'S PROOF

Frederic Remington's
"Exploring
the Lakes"

From the life of Pierre
Radisson, who voyaged
west of Lake Superior
to Lake Winnipeg

RIGHT:

I selected a floral print for the Merillats' bedcover, with the peony as the main flower against a neutral gold background. Stripes are one of my favorite decorating common denominators: they go with everything. Not only do they work in all types of fabric, they work especially well on a wall when hanging artwork.

TOP:

In Lynette's dressing room, I decided the idea was shoes, shoes, shoes. The upholstered chair in the shape of a high-heel shoe was the perfect fit.

LEFT:

The Victorian-style bedroom chaise has a channeled back in different shades of green velvet, from chartreuse to mint. Lynette's collection of antique hand mirrors is hung on the wall just above.

THIS PAGE:
One of the many guest rooms in
the house is filled with Lynette's
collection of antique wicker
pieces. For the floor I chose a
wool carpet with a rose border
named the Jacqueline Kennedy
"Camelot" rug, inspired by one
in the White House created for
the Kennedys by the decorator
Sister Parish, who was a first
cousin of Dorothy Draper.

OPPOSITE, CLOCKWISE FROM LEFT:
This room has a white-wicker
bench with a seat upholstered
in my pink-and-green OK Plaid.
It is placed against the lavender-
painted walls underneath a
portrait of Queen Elizabeth.

   Guests can rock away the
lazy days of July and August in
the two wicker rockers set next
to a summertime bay window.

   White organdy criss-cross
curtains set a light, airy tone for
the guest wing's Victorian-style
parlor. The wood-frame sofa,
which once had a dark stain,
is now bright white.

   Finding antique wicker
has been a passion of mine
over the years. This turn-of-the-
century chair is special for its
fanciful shape.

This skipper blue–painted den could be called the Admiral's Cove, as the paintings of ships on the walls and ship models placed about—everything a sea captain loves—indicate. What is now used as a serving dresser was once a sideboard in the mansion of John Jacob Astor on the Hudson River in New York State.

TOP:
Long before the actress
Esther Williams made swimming
glamorous, bathing costumes
were very basic. These suits
were found at the Grand Hotel's
annual antique show.

ABOVE AND RIGHT:
The lakeside entrance to the
ten-thousand-square-foot
boathouse is painted in my
Carleton Varney style, and
even the floor inside is made
of black-and-white squares
laid on the diagonal.

Of course, no color-filled fantasy house would be complete without a room with a secret door! The playroom and bedroom allow for all of the Merillats' grandchildren to sleep close together. The bunkbeds have blue spreads for the he's and pink spreads for the she's. The seven dwarfs are there too, lined up under the painted white-birch trees and aqua-blue sky of the walls.

LOVE MAKES OUR HOUSE A HOME

Yes, black and white are colors, too! When I first came to Dorothy Draper and Company, Inc., all of the conference chairs in Mrs. Draper's board room were upholstered in shiny patent leather with gold nail heads. By contrast, white linen has a summery feel. With this range of texture and tone, the possibilities are endless, especially when you add colorful artworks and brightly colored furniture in chartreuse and orange. Two of my residential projects use white walls as the background for their interior designs, which is very unlike me but well suited to the Nederlanders' home in Palm Beach and the Antons' apartment in Washington, D.C. In both residences, white was a reference to their sources of inspiration, from Modernism to Morocco.

A Moroccan Fantasy

Washington, D.C. is an international city, and home base for my well-traveled clients Patricia and William Anton, restaurateurs and culinary experts. I decided to create a Moroccan style for their penthouse apartment. We booked rooms at the famous Hôtel la Mamounia in Marrakech. We shopped in the souks and visited the Majorelle Garden for inspiration. I was affected by the clarity of the light in Morocco. Each city in each state in each country has its own light. Upon walking into the Antons' home, I wanted it to feel as though the entire apartment had been transported directly from Marrakech.

ABOVE:
The sit-down bar is covered in aqua-blue, rust-red, and golden-mustard ceramic tiles, purchased in Marrakech. The black-lacquer bar chairs from Kindel are a contemporary take on a Dorothy Draper design, with exotic leopard-print cushions.

LEFT:
A marble sculpture by the actor Anthony Quinn is placed on a pedestal I found in Morocco and set into a blue-, gold-, and black-tiled niche, a common element in Moorish architecture.

OPPOSITE:
An intricately hand-painted arched door brings an architectural element to the apartment. The black-marble floor is the perfect base for this exciting Moroccan wool rug. A foliage-motif frieze, often found in Moroccan homes, is painted along the crown molding in the living room.

Saffron, saffron—so North African

—in the living room.

PREVIOUS LEFT:

Many villas in Morocco have crisp white walls, and I decided this was what I would do in the living and dining areas. The floor-to-ceiling louvered shutters are in keeping with the open-air feel of the apartment, which is surrounded by terraces on all sides. The windows, unobstructed by draperies, bring in light. The purple-blue suede dining banquette, chairs with chartreuse seats and a pearlescent-white finish, and russet-red tablecloths complete the look in the dining room.

PREVIOUS RIGHT:

A small, white, carved-wood chest holds the Antons' flatware and table linens. The painting above the chest is something I came upon in the Palm Beach gallery owned by Jennifer Garrigues. The subject was fitting: a Moroccan village in the hills, with a mosque sitting on the highest peak, protecting the townspeople. I loved the colors—desert sand, sky blue, and green. Colorful artwork can bring all of the design elements in a room together.

THESE PAGES:

A saffron-orange velour fabric covers the furniture surrounding a coffee table made from a Moroccan door. A graphic black-on-white cut-velvet fabric is used on the throw cushions. Even the details of the raised ceiling reiterate the Moorish arch design of the window and door shutters.

OPPOSITE:

The star of this small den and dressing room is the wood and plaster ceiling, which was made on-site. Thousands of tiles were assembled by master craftsmen flown over from Morocco. My palette for the room included all the colors of the Moroccan culture: green, gold, red, pink, orange, and lavender.

TOP:

We found this light fixture in a souk in Marrakech. Here it is hung from the center of a sun-wheel design in the ceiling cove.

RIGHT:

A detail of a small cabinet in the room also shows the labor-intensive handiwork that was accomplished.

When visiting the Antons, guests stay in this elegant bedroom furnished with an inlaid mother-of-pearl headboard and night tables. I chose one of my very favorite colors—peacock blue—for the lamps, which have vibrant garnet-red shades. There is nothing like the light from a colored lamp shade to provoke intimacy and excitement in a bedroom, making for happy guests.

ABOVE:

A variety of pillows in luxurious fabrics, from florals to solids, are placed on the bed. The bedcover is monogrammed with the Antons' initials, and was handmade in Italy by the English linen firm Edi-B, whose shop in London caters to palaces in the Middle East.

Stylish Elegance

In Palm Beach, for theatrical producers and theatre owners Charlene and James Nederlander, I combined the decorating styles from their different residences into one elegant home done almost entirely in black and white. In one room, the horn chairs as well as a cowboy painting from their Arizona house are brought together with a white-marble mantelpiece, black-marble pedestals, and a newly acquired Joaquim Ruiz Millet Manuscript Rug. The Oriental vases, from another past life, add a stylish Asian touch. A black-and-white palette is often associated with Modernism and a mix of Eastern and Western influences. Both live harmoniously in this room, and the Nederlanders loved the look when they saw it.

THIS PAGE:

For the draperies and club chairs I chose white linen for its resilience and ability to deflect heat—perfect for Palm Beach. The black piping on the chairs, contemporary rug, and black-lacquer round end table from my Dorothy Draper collection, along with a handcrafted white ceramic lamp by New York designer Christopher Spitzmiller, complete the story here.

OPPOSITE AND OVERLEAF:

The theme continues throughout the entrance way and first-floor sitting rooms. A black-and-white statement is easy to accomplish with furnishings upholstered in cool white linen and all the tables and accessories in black, including a small sculpture of a cowboy.

THIS PAGE:

An oil painting by Hunt Slonem hangs on the white wall of the living room. The birds in Slonem's artwork, along with the golden sunflowers, influenced my choice of gold- and gray-velvet accent pillows. Regency-style black-and-gold armchairs have seats and backs upholstered in a contemporary print of red, gold, blue, and pumpkin tones.

OPPOSITE:

Raffia chairs hug the dining-room table, which was placed so diners could enjoy the view of Florida's Intracoastal Waterway. Hanging above the table is a shell chandelier I found in an antique shop on Dixie Highway in West Palm Beach. The painting of two Spanish women dancing is reminiscent of the architect Addison Mizner's Mediterranean Revival style, which had such a strong influence on Palm Beach architecture.

OVERLEAF:

What is a Palm Beach house without hibiscus flowers? Pink, gold, and green on the curved-back Kindel sofa say sunshine all year round. Black lamps and a vintage black-lacquer Dorothy Draper table are important details in this setting, as are the Nederlanders' French bergères.

In the fall of 2009, HSN approached me about creating a collection of home décor and furnishings called Carleton Varney Live Vividly, because of my colorful interiors. Two years later, a television show of the same name is still on the air every six weeks for several live viewings. This is not my first time on TV; I've been on other shows, such as *Good Morning America* and *Oprah*. But being on HSN is different. It is a continuous flow of dialogue. People call in with their stories about the pleasure they get out of decorating with color, and I have the opportunity to respond with my view of color's special power.

HSN produces everything they sell, so I work directly with their creative and merchandising teams. I send in my designs to be okayed, then they send samples for me to change or approve. Working together, it can take up to a year and a half to prepare a new item.

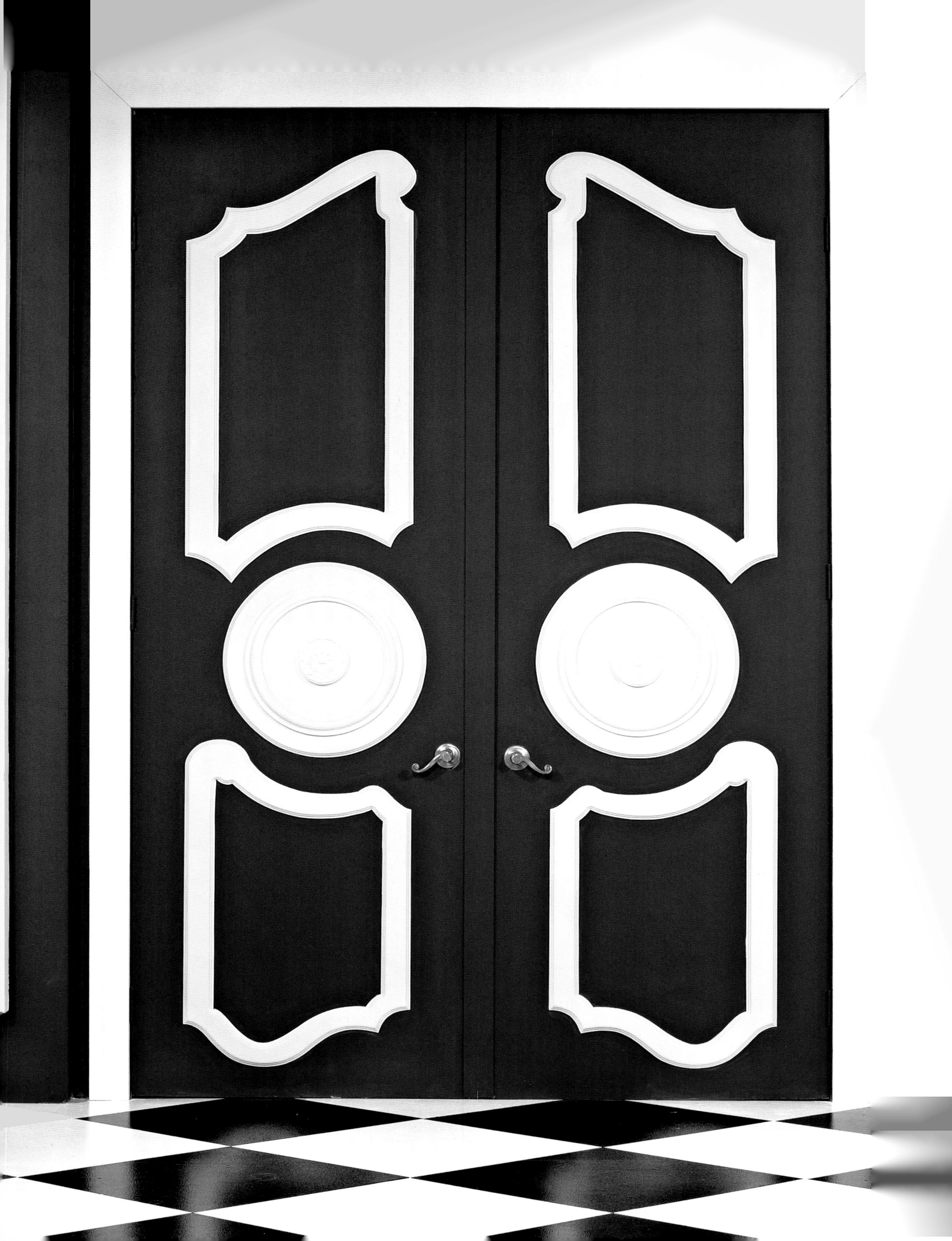

958-610
**Carleton Varney
400 Thread Count
Hillandale Rose
Sheet Set**
Retail Value
$76.50
HSN Price
$59.95
S&H $7.22
3 flex $19.98
800·284·3100
HSN.COM

30 day money back guarantee

Inspired by movies in the age of Marilyn Monroe, each one of my sets has a different theme.

Most shows on television have stages that are gray and drab, but my sets for *Live Vividly* are the opposite. I open with an image of my doorway, painted a different eye-catching color each time. For today's taping, it is forest green and white. The style replicates a famous door that Dorothy Draper created for the Camellia House in Chicago. Dorothy painted hers black and used versions of the same design in many projects.

PREVIOUS PAGES:

Trellis is one of my sheet patterns and it is available in six different colors. I have always been influenced by the figure of Thomas Jefferson and the trellis-like balustrades on his porches at Monticello.

I am on the set with Bobbi Ray Carter, one of the original hosts on HSN. She has been with the company for more than twenty-five years, and viewers trust her opinion. Here, I am telling her about my comforter set, which includes an assortment of pillow covers. I named this pattern Hillandale Rose after my farm in Upstate New York.

I am never ill-at-ease in front of the camera and feel like I am on stage. As a child, I took every kind of acting lesson, so performing feels natural to me. Part of the appeal of the show are the personalities of the callers and the stories they tell.

I redecorate the sets for every show. On one episode, I used a fifteen-inch blue-and-white-striped background for the ten-piece pink-and-white Hillandale Rose comforter set.

OVERLEAF:

Television-set decorating has become one of my special loves. Every set has three or four furniture groupings, each with a different background and featuring new products, such as pillows, rugs, headboards, and lamps. The host and I move from set to set, and over a two-day period, I can shoot eight live shows.

LEFT:

On the show, I make sure fresh flowers are part of the display. The bright color of the yellow roses adds excitement.

OPPOSITE:

I used one of my favorite patterns, Fudge Apron, as the starting point for a lovely set of china. My tableware for HSN is called Greenbrier Garden, and the design is a combination of flowers, stripes, and swags.

Fabric Index

Rhododendron: White
Carleton Varney By the Yard
100% Cotton

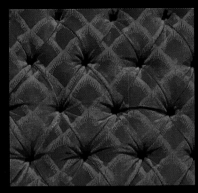

Rhulmann: Red
Carleton V Ltd.
68% Viscose, 24% Cotton, 8% Polyester

Baroque Bouquet: Black
Carleton Varney By the Yard
100% Cotton

Plantation High Performance: Berry
Carleton V Ltd.
100% Bella Dura

Chevron Check: Blue
Carleton V Ltd.
100% Cotton

Big Fish: Royal/White
Carleton Varney By the Yard
100% Cotton

Malibu: Black on White
Carleton V Ltd.
75% Linen, 25% Cotton

Tiger
Carleton Varney By the Yard
100% Polyester

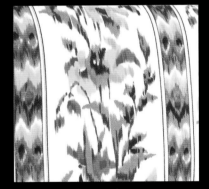

Santany: Aqua
Carleton Varney By the Yard
100% Cotton

Cymbidium Orchid: Pink
Carleton Varney By the Yard
100% Cotton

Camino Real: Pink/Green
Carleton Varney By the Yard
100% Cotton

Fudge Apron
Carleton Varney By the Yard
100% Cotton

In 1973, I established Carleton V Ltd., a textile design company that not only works with new designers to develop innovative fabrics and wall coverings but also represents my own line, Carleton Varney By the Yard, which includes some of Dorothy Draper's most famous designs. My former wife, Suzanne, was president of the company for more than twenty years and she brought my son Sebastian into the business. He in turn has added his own fresh vision to Carleton V Ltd.

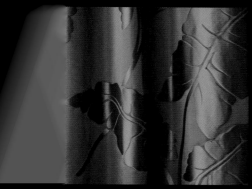

Copacabana: Jungle
Carleton V Ltd.
63% Polyester, 37% Silk

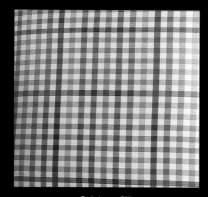

Rainbow Silk
Carleton Varney By the Yard
100% Silk

Tarkington Hall
Carleton Varney By the Yard
100% Cotton

Cymbidium Orchid: White
Carleton Varney By the Yard
100% Cotton

Boca Grande: Aqua
Carleton V Ltd.
55% Cotton, 45% Linen

Delphine: Coral
Carleton V Ltd.
78% Cotton, 22% Silk

Cane: Blue
Carleton Varney By the Yard
100% Cotton

Basket of Flowers: Purple/Yellow
Carleton Varney By the Yard
100% Cotton

Shannon Stripe: Blue/White
Carleton Varney By the Yard
100% Cotton

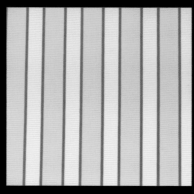

Index

Bibliography

Carter, Rosalynn. *First Lady from Plains.* Fayetteville, AK: University of Arkansas Press, 1994.

Conte, Robert. *The History of the Greenbrier.* Missoula, MT: Pictorial Histories Publishing, 2000.

Crater, Susan Bartlett and Libby Cameron. *Sister Parish Design: On Decorating.* New York, NY: St. Martin's Press, 2009.

Crawford, Joan. *My Way of Life.* New York, NY: Simon and Schuster, 1971.

Draper, Dorothy. *Decorating is Fun: How to be Your Own Decorator.* New York, NY: Pointed Leaf Press, 2007.

———. *Entertaining is Fun: How to be a Popular Hostess.* New York, NY: Rizzoli, 2004.

Eerdmans, Emily Evans. *Regency Redux, High Style Interiors, Napoleonic, Classical Moderne, and Hollywood Regency.* New York, NY: Rizzoli, 2008.

Foulkes, Nick. *The Carlyle.* New York, NY: Assouline, 2007.

Gray, Susan. Ed. *Designers on Designers: The Inspiration Behind Great Interiors.* New York, NY: McGraw-Hill, 2004.

Gura, Judith. *New York Interior Design, 1935-1985, Vol. 1: Inventors of Tradition.* New York, NY: Acanthus Press, 2008.

———. *New York Interior Design, 1935-1985, Vol. II: Masters of Modernism.* New York, NY: Acanthus Press, 2008.

Heller, Joseph. *Good as Gold.* New York, NY: Simon and Schuster, 1977.

Janjigian, Robert. *"Mr. Color."* Design Times Dec. 1998-Jan. 1999: 94-101.

Kelley, Kitty. *Nancy Regan: The Unauthorized Biography.* New York, NY: Simon and Schuster, 1971.

Read, Mimi. *"A Lakeside Cottage Goes from Classic to Wild."* House Beautiful Feb. 2009: 88–98

Russell, Margaret: *Designing Women: Interiors by Leading Style Makers.* New York, NY: Stewart Tabori & Chang, 2001.

Stovall, Colleen. *"The King of Color."* Mackinac Living Vol IV 2004: 26-34.

Varney, Carleton. *"Carleton Varney's 40 Shades of Green."* Social & Personal July 1996: 60-64.

———. *Carleton Varney's ABCs of Decorating.* New York, NY: E.P. Dutton, 1983.

———. *Carleton Varney Decorates from A to Z: An Encyclopedia of Home Decoration.* Indianapolis and New York: Bobbs-Merrill Company, Inc., 1977.

———. *Carleton Varney Decorates Windows.* Des Moines, IA: Meredith Corporation, 1975.

———. *"Carleton Varney Sees Red."* Social & Personal Nov. 1996: 62-66.

———. *Color Magic.* New York, NY: E.P. Dutton, 1985.

———. *"Color Makes a Home Sparkle."* Palm Beach Daily News 13 Aug. 2009: B4.

———. *Decorating with Color.* Des Moines, IA: Meredith Corporation, 1972.

———. *Down Home: America's Country Decorating Book.* Indianapolis and New York: Bobbs-Merrill Company, Inc., 1984.

———. *The Draper Touch: The High Life and High Style of Dorothy Draper.* New York, NY: Shannongrove Press, 1988.

———. *Houses in My Heart.* New York, NY: Pointed Leaf Press, 2008.

———. *In the Pink: Dorothy Draper: America's Most Fabulous Decorator.* New York, NY: Pointed Leaf Press, 2006.

———. *"Pumpkin: a Decorating Hue That's Perfect for Palm Beach Homes."* Palm Beach Daily News 30 Oct. 2009: 8.

———. *"Rich Cranberry Delightful in Sauce, on Walls."* Palm Beach Daily News 11 Dec. 2009: 6

———. *"Your Rooms Will Sparkle When Deep Purple Calls."* Palm Beach Daily News 31 July 2008: B6

*T*o the memory of my parents, Julia and Carleton Sr., who introduced me
to coloring books at a young age. I did not realize then how I would be
influenced by happy colors, nor did I realize how color would affect the lives
of my sons, Nicholas, Seamus, and Sebastian.

Acknowledgments

Thanks to the following associates and colleagues for all the help they have given me in the preparation of this book.

Brinsley Matthews, my director of Design and Operations, who had an idea of this "book to be" before it was born, and who coordinates the design projects of Dorothy Draper and Company, Inc., both here and abroad.

Jane Creech, my editor and organizer, without whose interest and passion this book would never have taken shape.

Michel Arnaud, for his creative genius behind the camera in making the specially commissioned photographs of each project, and to Michel's assistant, Pawel Kaminski.

Designers Joel Avirom and Jason Snyder, for giving this book its truly unique style.

Anne Hellman White, our copy editor, who took my words and made them flow, while at the same time dotting the i's and crossing the t's.

Nellie Xinos, in my New York office, who did all the secretarial coordination, including the typing of my hard-to-read longhand. Also to my staff members who worked on the book: Susan van Berg, my executive assistant; Sara Beaudry; Alex Goyfman; Patricia Justice; Marlon Logan; and Dan Parker.

Thank you to Ernest Fox, who has worked with me as an illustrator from my very first year at Dorothy Draper and Company, Inc.

I would like to acknowledge these people for their help in making the book a reality: Jennifer Byrant, Bobbi Ray Carter, Debra Castellano, Mike Cathey, Cynthia Crippen, Heather Cusick, Kathy Greif, Scott Haberkorn, Ashley Lutzenkirchen, Thomas McCarthy, Rhoda Miller, Sharyn Post, Nancy Reeser, Pam Rhodes, Brett Rousse, Katherine Sharpe, Shannon Smith, and Mery Zamata. And to Mimi Cunningham for the beautiful flowers at the Grand Hotel.

I am especially grateful to my friends and clients Nancy Abraham and Arnold Moss, Therese Carreon, Kyle Crews, Mindy Grossman (CEO of HSN), Lynette and Richard Merillat, Amelia and Dan Musser, Charlene and James Nederlander, Sandy and Richard Roberts, and Francie Whittenburg.

My sincere appreciation to my son Sebastian Varney and his staff at Carleton V Ltd., Brittney Bean and Katie Crider, for their assistance. I also thank Jane West of Carleton Varney By the Yard in Palm Beach.

I extend my greatest thanks to Jim and Kathy Justice, owners of the Greenbrier. Jim has given me his trust to continue a legacy of vivid color.

JACKET COVER:
Color is part of my personal style. I am rarely without a colorful scarf
or bandana around my neck. My socks are red in honor of my friend
and client Van Johnson, who always wore them.

CASE COVER:
These pink and red hand-painted roses were specially commissioned
for the Greenbrier Casino Club entrance.

FRONT AND BACK ENDPAPERS:
I've never met a color I didn't like. My world has been made up of
some wonderful adventures. I've been an observer and creator
of many colorful places, homes, rooms, fabrics, carpet designs,
and furniture pieces. Together they have become a part of my
kaleidoscope of memories and experiences.

HALF TITLE:
Flowers and trees produce nature's colors all year round. As a
designer, it is my work to capture and bring these elements into our
lives at home. I am holding a crystal paperweight that sits on my desk
and inspires me in every season.

TITLE PAGE AND CONTENTS PAGE:
I am on the set of my show *Live Vividly*, on HSN. My gestures, in
decorating and on the air, are like those of a conductor, bringing all
of the style notes together to make a melody. Color and music both
play an important role in filling a room with happiness.

FOLLOWING PAGE:
Here I am in the soon-to-be-restored Merchant's House, part of the
Royal Palace of Lithuania, where we have acted as the design and
decorating consultants on the project. Now a liberated city, Vilnius
was occupied by the Russians, the Nazis, and the Soviets. It is an
ancient city and the birthplace of my maternal grandparents. I have
returned to roots that I never thought I would see or feel.

PHOTOGRAPHY CREDITS:
Unless otherwise noted below, all images were taken by Michel
Arnaud on location with assistance from Pawel Kaminski. Every effort
has been made to locate copyright holders. Any omission will be
corrected in future editions.

© Ron Blunt Photography Architecture, Interiors, & Landscape
ronbluntphoto.com: 16 (top, left)

Photograph by Bruce Buck/*Architectural Digest* © Condé Nast:
16 (second from the top, right)

Photography by Richard Champion: 14 (top, left)

Photograph by Derry Moore: 232

James Moritz Photography www.jamesmoritz.com email: Info@
jamesmoritz.com: 10

Photo by Peter Vitale: 16 (bottom, right)

© 2011 Carleton Varney

ISBN: 978-0-615-45090-2

Library of Congress number: 2011903829

Inquiries should be sent to:

Shannongrove Press
60 East 56th Street, 10th Floor
New York, NY 10022

Printed and bound in China

First Edition

10 9 8 7 6 5 4 3 2 1

A Rooster Books Production for
SHANNONGROVE PRESS
NEW YORK